Blessings for Church Occasions

Ruth C. Ikerman

Abingdon Press

Blessings for Church Occasions

Copyright © 1987 by Abingdon Press

All rights reserved.
No part of this work may be reproduced or transmitted in any form or by any means, electronic or mechanical, including photocopying and recording, or by any information storage or retrieval system, except as may be expressly permitted by the 1976 Copyright Act or in writing from the publisher. Requests for permission should be addressed in writing to Abingdon Press, 201 8th Avenue South, Nashville, TN 37202.

ISBN 687-03624-0

MANUFACTURED BY THE PARTHENON PRESS AT
NASHVILLE, TENNESSEE, UNITED STATES OF AMERICA

To my adopted sister,
Edith Fisher Gamber,
with affection and appreciation.

PREFACE

The first telephone call of the morning was from an acquaintance who said, "I have to give the blessing at our meeting today, and I wonder if you have one already written down that I can use."

The request was not unusual, because I have discovered, from some thirty years of writing devotional books, that many people with active prayer lives of their own hesitate to give a blessing for a group affair.

So the purpose of this book is to help people express what is in their hearts when they face church situations that call for public blessings. An introductory paragraph describes the specific situation, followed by the suggested blessing.

May God bless each of us as we live our busy lives in our hometown churches.

Ruth C. Ikerman

CONTENTS

Blessing for an Annual Church Dinner............. 9
Blessing for Sunday School........................... 11
Blessing for a Stewardship Meeting................13
Blessings for Missionary Meetings...................15
   Foreign Mission Blessing............................ 15
   Home Mission Blessing............................... 16
Blessing for a Choir Supper........................... 17
Blessing for Monthly Group Meetings............ 19
Blessing for a Bible Study Class.....................20
Blessing for a Teacher Training Session........... 21
Blessing for Administrative Sessions...............22
Blessings for Lay Leaders............................. 23
   For Our Church... 23
   For Our Pastor... 24
Blessings for Informal Outdoor Meetings........ 25
   Worship Service... 25
   Church Picnic...26
Blessing for a Women's Membership Coffee.... 27
Blessing for a Women's Springtime Festival.... 29
Blessing for a Mother-Daughter Banquet.........31
Blessing for a Father-Son Event...................... 33
Blessing for Athletic Events...........................35
Blessing for a Church Library Meeting........... 36
Blessing for Graduation Recognition...............38
Blessing for Craft Class Projects.....................40
Blessing for a Yearly Church Retreat.............. 41

Blessing for a Church Anniversary.................43
Blessings for Christmas Events......................45
　　Women's Christmas Breakfast....................45
　　Sunday School Christmas Party..................46
Blessing for a New Year Event......................47
A Blessing of Benediction............................48

BLESSING FOR AN ANNUAL CHURCH DINNER

Many churches have yearly banquets when reports of progress are given and plans are made for the new year. This is often a time of spiritual sentiment for the members who attend and an opportunity to greet newcomers. The shut-ins need to be remembered; sometimes flowers from the tables are carried to them by designated committees. Thus the invocation calls for an all-embracing approach to the various ages and interests of the congregation.

Our dear loving heavenly Father, we are grateful for this opportunity of Christian fellowship with one another and with thee. Please be very near this night to our dear shut-ins who are not able to meet with us physically, but whose hearts join with ours in hope and love for this church. We remember with warm hearts also the men and women who have shared our spiritual dreams and who are now gone from this earthly life.

We ask thee to give us an abiding sense of thy own continuous presence in times of change. May we each take from the past the blessing of joyous memories, and grant that the inspiration of this gathering may give us fresh energy for future activities in thy kingdom.

Bless this food to our bodies and this fellowship

to our hearts that we may serve thee better in our homes, through this church, and in our community and nation. These mercies we ask in the precious name of thy son, Jesus, our Lord and our Savior. Amen.

BLESSING FOR SUNDAY SCHOOL

Perhaps the most universally known department of the church is that of the Sunday school. From its classes have come many of the current church leaders, who in turn are concerned that present plans provide for the needs of students living in a constantly changing world. Methods of teaching may change, and the approach to solutions may vary; yet the essential problems of learning right from wrong and establishing good Christian habits of service remain the same through the generations. A substantial prayer life sustains and undergirds the goals and projects of any Sunday school.

Dear Lord, hear our thanks for the pupils of this Sunday school and for the families they represent. We pray in gratitude also for the teachers and administrators of this department of our church. All of us stand in need of thy constant presence in helping us plan and carry out programs and lessons that will build Christian character and personality. Accept our gratitude for teachers of the past who have kept this Sunday school intact with their dedicated Sunday to Sunday service. Give to us an enlarged vision of our opportunities to grow by reaching out to newcomers in this community. May no one feel a stranger in our midst, but always welcomed to the house of God through the open doors of our Sunday school. Help us to know how to use thy eternal truths in solving modern problems as we all grow in grace. In Jesus' name, Amen.

BLESSING FOR A STEWARDSHIP MEETING

The time spent on setting up a budget and determining how to raise necessary funds is an important part of the yearly program of any church with growing outreach. Such a meeting may follow the morning church service or may take the form of an evening dinner given over exclusively to the presentation of facts and figures. Whatever the choice of time, encourage the view of stewardship as a vital part of the church program through a stewardship blessing.

Dear God, we would be willing stewards of thy bounty, ever grateful for the abundance of goodness which comes into our hearts from thee. We are aware of the great gifts of health and energy to work day by day and for the natural blessings of earth, air, and water. Forgive us for the times we have taken these elements for granted, forgetting that thou art the giver of every good and perfect gift.

Now as we come together to consider our stewardship of such gifts, place in our hearts generous motives of unselfish giving as reflections of thy wondrous gifts to us. Grant us wisdom to know how best to share our financial blessings with other persons that they may be encouraged to live

Christian lives and, in turn, may be enabled to bless others and to serve thee better.

From this discussion, may we all come away with renewed appreciation of our daily blessings and fresh strength to find Christian solutions to today's problems. Amen.

BLESSINGS FOR MISSIONARY MEETINGS

With the arrival of the space age and frequent air travel, the far places of the world have come closer to the hometown church. Changes in transportation bring mission speakers to local areas with greater frequency than in former years. Contact with those so recently on the mission field imparts fresh perspective to mission committees and missionary meetings. If not in actual presence of the missionaries, at least in letters that arrive swiftly by air mail, the church can keep abreast of current needs for supplies and funds. Reading such letters aloud provides interesting missionary programs for youth and adults in the hometown church. An appropriate mission blessing can motivate involvement in and giving to mission causes. Here are two suggestions—one for foreign mission and another for home mission projects.

Foreign Mission Blessing

Dear God, we are mindful of the Bible's admonition to go and teach all nations and of the precious promise of thy presence with all who go in thy name to serve in foreign fields. Keep us ever aware of our ability to make our influence felt as Christians through the support we give to such mission projects. May we never forget the need for daily prayer to encourage and sustain those who serve in mission fields. May this interest be backed by our financial resources to the best of our budget's ability.

Give us guidance as we plan our giving in the light of the many needs of thy world. May our hearts be so enlarged as to include others in our prayers and activities. Keep us from limited vision and expand our horizons to include Christian brothers and sisters in far corners of thy great world. Together may we all give thee praise for thy wondrous blessings of peace in the heart and, ultimately, in the world. Amen.

Home Mission Blessing

Dear God, we thank thee for the blessings of our homes and families as well as for this church. Even as we count the abundance of thy goodness to us, we are aware that there are others in this area who lack food, clothing, and adequate shelter. Deliver us from self-centered interest in our own welfare, and open our eyes to our opportunities for Christian activities near our homes. Give us wisdom and tact to do gracious acts in humility as we sense the responsibility for neighborly service. Help us remember all needy hearts as we plan our church outreach, and arrange our personal and joint budgets. Give us sharing hearts and outstretched hands to serve thee through home missions. Amen.

BLESSING FOR A CHOIR SUPPER

Attending choir practice on a weekly basis represents consistent service to the church and often results in firm friendships among members who sing together for any length of time. Some churches make a habit of entertaining the choir once a year to try to say "Thank You" for weekly service in song. Other choirs organize their own potluck suppers and meet more frequently for the pleasure of informal contacts prior to their rehearsals. There are many blessings that choir groups may choose to sing at such affairs, but here is a prose blessing for use in calling such a group together.

Kind Lord, precious Lord, be very near to us as we gather in happy fellowship with choir members of our own church. Let harmony reign in all our hearts as together we partake of these blessings of food and conversation.

We thank thee for the opportunities we have to carol thy praises in weekly services, leading others to know the beauty and power of the precious heritage of church music. Let us always be aware of music as a ministry for present needs. May our music be extended into the lives of those who listen, that they may be encouraged when discouraged, strengthened when weak, and always enabled to face life anew with a song in their hearts.

Keep our voices and our lives in harmony with thy will. Amen.

BLESSING FOR MONTHLY GROUP MEETINGS

It is customary in many churches for certain groups to meet on a monthly basis, whether committees, families, singles, young people, the elderly, or those with special interests, such as missions or crafts. Usually some member has the responsibility of calling the group together before business or social activities. Here is a suggested monthly blessing.

Dear Father, as the time for our monthly meeting arrives, we are aware of how quickly the days and weeks speed past. We are grateful that we can meet today with our common interest in mind. Help us to make wise use of the time allotted for consideration of our business that thy kingdom may be advanced by our activities in this area. Undergird our deliberations with a spirit of unity and with a deep desire to serve thee better everyday. Grant each heart here a blessing to carry home to enrich the days of work and play until we meet again. May each month find us further along on our journey of faith. In Jesus' name, Amen.

BLESSING FOR A BIBLE STUDY CLASS

Even a comparatively small group meeting for Bible study may need a special blessing to open the study period. It is helpful if students can supply this without always relying on the pastor or class teacher. In fact, the Bible study class makes an ideal place for the timid to begin to practice giving public blessings. Here is a simple, brief introductory prayer written at the request of one of the men enrolled for the first time in a Bible study class. He used it once and thereafter was able to give an original blessing freely from his own heart.

Dear God, we thank thee for this opportunity to learn about the Bible with the help of our fine pastor and teacher. Show us how to make the most of the time we spend together so that we may gain information and inspiration to live our lives better. We are grateful to be able to spend time with friends in this class and to have a chance to make new ones. Bless this class and our church. We ask this in Jesus' name. Amen.

BLESSING FOR A TEACHER TRAINING SESSION

One of the most valuable tools of the Sunday school is a teacher training session in which experienced and new teachers meet together to update their methods of teaching. Studying problems together often generates new solutions. Sometimes the most modern methods are improved by studied appreciation of what has worked in the past. There is power in the knowledge that teachers are praying for one another, even as they ask blessings on all the students in the various classes.

Lord, we remember the times our Savior taught his disciples by the seaside, and we are grateful for that loving leadership that has come down to us across the centuries. Humbly we ask thee to provide wisdom and guidance for the leaders of this group and for each seeker here. Help us to know that together we sit at the feet of the Master Teacher when we read our Bibles and, through our prayer lives, seek for greater skill to reach others.

Please work on the hearts of our students as well as all of us as teachers so that together we may have a fresh vision of the wonders of thy word and its power to change lives for the better.

Grant us the simplicity of mind to accept the glorious concepts of Christian teaching for our own lives. Thus may we be enabled to express thy truth to benefit others. In Jesus name, Amen.

BLESSING FOR ADMINISTRATIVE SESSIONS

Because the persons who are selected to administer the various church boards are usually well qualified in their chosen fields, the tendency of many church members is to take their service for granted. After all, such persons are used to making decisions in their homes, businesses, and professions. Yet they have a real need for the remainder of the church to pray for them in reaching decisions and putting plans into action. Here is a blessing for use as administrators undertake the organization of churchwide projects of service.

Father, you know our hearts. We feel privileged to hold positions of leadership in this church, but at the same time are humbled by our responsibilities.

Certain problems face us in various areas of this church, and we feel a definite need for thy divine guidance. As our individual prayers ascend to thee for wisdom in making decisions, grant us an overview of the entire picture that we may have a vision of what thou would have us accomplish in this community. Let our outreach grow to those who do not as yet know thee as Lord.

May our own lives reflect thy glory as we try to use our talents to the best of our abilities to extend thy kingdom. Grant us the wisdom to plan correctly and the courage to accomplish much, that we may grant thee the praise that is due thee always. Amen.

BLESSINGS FOR LAY LEADERS

One of the most important jobs in any church is that undertaken by the lay leader. Often the church members look to that person for guidance in setting policies and for wisdom in knowing how to carry them out in church emergencies. The influence of the lay leader extends into many areas, including that of helping create the devotional atmosphere of church groups. The lay leader may be expected to give blessings on various occasions, growing out of personal prayer life and meditation. Here are two suggested prayers, a blessing for our church and a blessing for our pastor.

Lay Leader Blessing for Our Church

Dear God, as a church we are grateful for one another and for our opportunities of service for thee. From our appreciation of one another and from our remembrance of thy blessings in the lives of each of us, we gather strength for the tasks facing our home church. Help us to become aware that what we do here may assist thy world to more ably face the challenges of this generation. May we ever be aware of the world situations that call for strength and courage, and thus give our best to the activities of this church. Keep our hearts pure and our minds clearly focused on thee, that we may serve thee better in our personal lives, in our homes, and in this church family. In Jesus' name, Amen.

Lay Leader Blessing for Our Pastor

Dear Father, we come to thee with thankful hearts for the devoted service of our dedicated pastor. So often we have been helped by pastoral prayers for our welfare as we have met for Sunday services. We remember also the compassionate prayers at times of great personal crises of illness or death in the family. Just now we would reciprocate these prayers with grateful hearts when we ask thy blessing on our pastor and all those dear to the pastor's heart. Grant refreshing strength for renewed service as we all reach out with prayers to increase our joy in serving thee. In Jesus' name, Amen.

BLESSINGS FOR INFORMAL OUTDOOR MEETINGS

Particularly in the summertime, many churches organize at least one informal outdoor meeting—often several. This may take the form of a swimming party for young people at the home of one of the members, or it may mean a trip to a city park for a picnic of a ride to a nearby stream where cool breezes invite friendly games of ball or sack races. Such settings offer opportunity for picnics and for outdoor vesper services. These may include singing familiar songs or a brief talk based, perhaps, on one of the beloved psalms. A blessing to open or conclude the meeting contributes to its purpose. Here are two blessings, a blessing for an outdoor worship service and a blessing for a church picnic.

Blessing for an Outdoor Worship Service

God of the open air, we come to thee grateful for the outdoors and all that it offers in the way of recreation and pleasure to all ages. We thank thee also for our church, with its regular routine, and the members with whom we may share this informal outdoor fellowship.

Help us all to relax and to know that we are indeed thy children, welcome in all thy world to enjoy the beauty of mountains, seashore, desert, trees, and flowers. In this relaxed setting, may our minds be free from trivia and clutter, so that we may see clearly our opportunities to serve thee better. Grant us fresh energy and renewed zest for the projects of our church, because we have taken this time to worship thee in this natural setting. Bless each of us and our church so that we may reach others for thee. Amen.

Blessing for a Church Picnic

Dear Father, hear our thanks for each home represented here. As we partake of food together, may it be as a united church family, one in hopes and aspiration and thoroughly dedicated to the welfare of each person present. Please bless, also, our absent dear ones as we remember the food and fellowship of other occasions. Keep us all within the circle of thy loving arms, that we may embrace others in Christian fellowship. Amen.

BLESSING FOR A WOMEN'S MEMBERSHIP COFFEE

Women's groups in churches sometimes hold a yearly coffee to attract and enlist new members and to help the existing members to become better acquainted with one another and with newcomers. Such a meeting provides an opportunity to hand out the year books, to receive pledges, and to announce the theme for the year's programs. Seasonal flowers on the serving table provide appropriate decoration. Even such informal affairs are given better focus with a blessing before the line forms at the refreshment table, where cookies and nutbread sandwiches await for delightful sociability.

Our loving heavenly Father, we thank thee for the privilege of meeting together again as the fall season begins. We are aware this morning that some of our dear ones who were with us in the springtime have left their earthly homes during this summer season. We thank thee for the memory of their service with us, and we ask thee humbly to restore to us the happy memories of their smiles and their loving presence.

Grant to each of us here today fresh energy for the tasks that lie ahead. May this be a year of rich fellowship with one another and with thee. Give us guidance to do thy will in our largest projects and in our smallest acts of devotion.

Bless this food to our bodies and this fellowship to our hearts. These mercies we ask in the precious name of Jesus Christ, our Lord and our Savior. Amen.

BLESSING FOR A WOMEN'S SPRINGTIME FESTIVAL

Many women's groups have at least one large event during the year, and springtime is often chosen for the occasion. Women of other churches may be invited by their friends to attend a salad luncheon or a brunch with food served at tables for four, or at longer tables, with special decorations. All such events call for an introductory blessing, and whenever asked to write one, I try to learn the theme and incorporate that into the wording. Because our church is located in the citrus area, we call our event the Annual Citrus Festival. Other areas use other fruits, flowers, or vegetables around which to organize their local festival. Given here is a generalized blessing built around the theme of springtime.

Our loving heavenly Father, we are grateful for this renewed opportunity for fellowship with friends of many churches. As we gather to celebrate springtime, let it be with joyous hearts, glad for the returning promise of each new spring. If the chill of winter has entered our homes because of illness or sorrow, may these shadows be removed as we sense the reassuring sunshine of thy eternal love. Even as the surrounding groves and fields give nourishing fruits and vegetables to the world, may our lives grow to fruition in golden acts of Christian service. Bless now this food and this fellowship that we may serve thee better in the days ahead. These mercies we ask in the name of thy Son Jesus, our Lord and our Savior. Amen.

BLESSING FOR A MOTHER-DAUGHTER BANQUET

One of the most joyous occasions of the year in many churches is the annual Mother-Daughter Banquet, open to all women of the church. While it is true that not all women qualify as mothers, it is also true that all the women of the church are surely daughters. Therefore, the occasion often unites women of all ages—those who are full-time homemakers, career people, and those who balance home and office. Here is a suggested blessing to use at the table before the banquet is served, the toasts given, and the program presented.

Dear God, we thank thee for this joyous opportunity for rich fellowship with thee and with one another. We ask a special blessing on each heart here and on our absent dear ones.

Let all of us have the sense of wonder that children know and the steadfastness of character that belongs to true maternal hearts everywhere. Grant that from this happy occasion we may draw energy and strength for the tasks of this troubled generation. Show us how to combine a vision of a peaceful future with wisdom to solve the many problems of the present age. May we remember always our precious heritage as Christian mothers and daughters.

Please bless this food to our bodies and this fellowship to our hearts, that we may all serve thee better in the days ahead. These mercies we ask in the name of thy Son Jesus, our Lord and our Savior. Amen.

BLESSING FOR A FATHER-SON EVENT

It is not so simple to organize a Father-Son Event as it was in days before divorce became so prevalent. Usually foster fathers must be found for some of the sons living with their mothers in single parent homes. Yet from such fleeting contacts as a Father-Son banquet, barbecue, or breakfast have come growing friendships between a boy and one of the men of the church who is willing to extend a helping hand. Sometimes a prominent sports figure can be secured to give a talk appealing to all ages. Efforts to make a Father-Son event inclusive of all the men and boys within the church family can result in valuable Christian contacts and expanding interest in such year-round group activities as the Sunday school.

Dear heavenly Father, we thank thee for this opportunity for fathers and sons to meet together in happy fellowship under the auspices of our church home. Let each of us be aware that we are indeed Sons of God, our heavenly Father, as we share the companionship of our own father or of an adopted father.

Help us to be better men and boys in future days because of the inspiration of this meeting. As we spend time together in fun and enjoying this food, may we realize anew the joys of living Christian lives and of partaking in the spiritual manna prepared for our use day by day through our jobs in the modern workplace and through our schools. Help us to return a portion of our substance and ourselves to the work of thy kingdom, serving thee better as fathers and sons. Amen.

BLESSING FOR ATHLETIC EVENTS

With the growing interest in developing a sound body through physical fitness, many churches place increasing attention on organized athletic events. Enthusiasm may grow within the entire church as a softball team of young people forms to participate in citywide games. Often through such activities a kinship develops among the players, which leads to enduring friendships. From such teams there develop leaders for future groups of young people. Undergirding such activities is the strength found in spiritual awareness through the use of prayer for good sportsmanship.

Dear God, we ask thee to be very close to each of us as we face the physical challenge of playing a good game with fine sportsmanship. We remember that Jesus grew in stature and in favor with God and man, and we would emulate this example. Help us to keep to the rules of the game, never cheating in an effort to win.

Let us know that true success comes in how we play the game with others, who may see in our example the ideal of good sportsmanship. Let nothing we do detract from the image of Christ we strive to express in our dealings with others. From this athletic contest may we learn new lessons of Christian living to take with us through life. Amen.

BLESSING FOR A CHURCH LIBRARY MEETING

Many church members enjoy reading as a happy hobby and help in forming church libraries from which books may be shared with all the families. A library committee on the lookout for books to be contributed to a central location can be one of the most helpful groups of the church and Sunday school. Such libraries often start on a small scale with a few books available on a table at the end of the morning service. As more books are donated, a special space may be selected to hold bookshelves. Ideally there are low tables and chairs at which small children can sit and browse through their picture books. A fine way to encourage library participation is to organize a dinner, with library use central to the theme and program. Here is a suggested invocation.

Dear God, we thank thee for the joy of this opportunity for fellowship with friends who love books and for the rich blessing of our association with books. We are grateful for all the gift of reading brings into our lives—ancient wisdom from the cherished past, pertinent help for the troubled present, and special dreams for a peaceful future. We thank thee, also, for today's speaker, who stimulates our minds and enriches our hearts. Please bless this food and all the aspects of our being together, that we may serve thee better in days ahead. We give thee our thanks and praise thy holy name. Amen.

BLESSING FOR GRADUATION RECOGNITION

With increasing emphasis on education, evidenced by extension classes for adults, the graduation banquet becomes an important part of the total church program. Not exclusively for youth, it can be a time of uniting all ages in the endeavor to learn more about today's world and how to solve its problems. Recognition can be granted at a church dinner with opportunity for personal congratulations following the meal. Some churches use one Sunday morning to call graduating students to the altar to receive congratulations. When an adult has achieved a degree after much special study, the entire family may be asked to stand with the graduate. In this age of many immigrants to the United States, you may want to congratulate adults for successfully learning English as a second language. From such encouragement comes motivation for new studies.

Dear Father, we come to this milestone in the lives of students with deep gratitude for the teachings of eternal truths in the Bible. We are grateful for this opportunity of fellowship that celebrates the achievements of the mind in learning about thy wonderful world. We remember with appreciation all the parents who were the first teachers of these students, even before they met their first school teachers. And we would not forget the dedicated Sunday school teachers who in their limited weekly times have taught the rules of Christian behavior. Grant that from this happy occasion we may all draw fresh strength for further study in our homes and churches, always taking advantage of the cultural opportunities of our communities. Thus may we serve thee with minds illuminated by knowledge and motivated by loving service. Bless this food and this fellowship to the furthering of thy kingdom. Amen.

BLESSING FOR CRAFT CLASS PROJECTS

A fairly new innovation in some churches is craft classes in which participants work on projects for shut-ins or other special groups. A project may be the making of tray favors for use in nursing homes at seasonal holidays. A church may establish a class with a more ambitious goal, such as learning painting, pottery, or weaving. Although often loosely organized, such craft sessions may be called together effectively with a blessing.

Dear God, as we come together to use our hands in service for thee, we ask a special blessing on all our activities designed for good. We are grateful that we have the energy to use our talents on behalf of those who may be unable to help themselves. We thank thee for the gifts and talents thou has given us.

May our work be but an outer expression of our inner prayers for the healing of the sick, the comforting of the bereaved, and the uplifting of those in need. As we work for others, may the projects of our hands serve as tranquilizers for our own problems as we try to serve thee better as Christians. Help us to be better co-workers with thee, finding joy in craft accomplishments. Amen.

BLESSING FOR A YEARLY CHURCH RETREAT

A yearly event in many successful churches is the annual retreat. As many of the church families as possible leave the hometown briefly to gather for fellowship and to set goals for the new year. This event calls for extensive work by the leaders and financial preparation that allows fees to be as low as possible. Committees for food, housing, and program do much background work before the time of departure. Much of the success of the time spent together depends on the spiritual tone established at the outset of the week-end.

Father of us all, be very near to this group as our church family gathers for a retreat to renew our spiritual strength and to plan ahead for future growth. We would not walk before thee, but ask thee humbly to lead us in all our discussions and in facing up to the problems and demands of the present age.

We are grateful for this opportunity to meet together away from the daily responsibilities of routine. Grant that from this fellowship may come new friendships and a heightened sense of our togetherness as Christians united in a common cause.

Let there be moments of lighthearted play and

pleasure to balance our serious discussions and our planning for future events. May this be a time of strengthened spiritual resolve to live daily lives that testify to thy power and saving grace. In Jesus' name, Amen.

BLESSING FOR A CHURCH ANNIVERSARY

When a church observes a special historical date, anything from a first to a one-hundredth anniversary, there is the need for a special invocation of blessing. It adds interest if this can include some brief mention of local or historical facts of importance. A young church can review its beginnings and significant accomplishments. Often "old-timers" of a long-established church can supply facts from the past and appreciate being asked by the one who is preparing the blessing. Here is the invocation I wrote when my hometown church celebrated its first hundred years. Fashion your own blessing with your church's history in mind.

Our dear heavenly Father, we thank thee for the great blessing of thy loving presence with this church across the changing years of a century of Christian service. We are grateful for the pioneer men and women who cared enough about the verities of eternity to found this church in a first building of worship. We remember the later sacrifices of time and talent so that more adequate facilities could be provided for their children and grandchildren to learn about God and how to live as Christians. Now, in the "Space Age," we ask anew for a special portion of thy power that we may never become indifferent to the values of Christian fellowship, with one another and with the other churches in our beloved city. Even as we celebrate the first one hundred years of commitment, help us to realize with humility our human frailties and to remember thy promise that a thousand years with thee are as but a day. Let our day be strengthened with the righteousness that comes from thee. Bless this food to our bodies and this fellowship to our hearts, and guide and direct us in rewarding years ahead. These mercies we ask in the name of thy Son, Jesus, our Lord and our Savior. Amen.

BLESSINGS FOR CHRISTMAS EVENTS

At Christmas there is always a need for a blessing for seasonal church affairs. Perhaps it is a traditional Sunday school party when gifts may be brought unwrapped to be given to a neighborhood settlement house, or it may be a women's breakfast or luncheon meeting when members are free to invite friends from other churches. Annually I write an invocation for a women's breakfast program, which features lovely decorations in the rose motif. At this time a pin in the shape of a rose is presented as "The Rose of Sharon Award" to a woman who has given generously of herself to the group during the preceding year. A reverent musical program sets a high tone of inspiration for the Christian season. Included here is a recent invocation written for such an event and a second blessing designed for a Sunday school party.

Blessing for a Women's Christmas Breakfast

Our dear kind loving heavenly Father, on this special occasion in the time of Christmas, we come humbly to thy throne of grace, asking for thy loving blessing. With women of many different churches represented here today we pray for a renewed understanding of thy universal love and compassion that we may all serve thee better. Grant that from this happy morning we may find vigor for the special errands of this season. Keep all of us and our absent dear ones in the light of thy healing love. Bless this food to our bodies and this fellowship to our hearts. And may we remember all year that Christmas is the reconciling of God and humanity through the coming of thy Son, Jesus Christ, our Lord and our Savior, in whose name we pray. Amen.

Blessing for a Sunday School Christmas Party

Dear God, at this happy season when we observe the birth of thy Son, Jesus, hear our thanks for the many precious memories of Christmas in our homes and in this church. Grant us a special portion of thy love as we meet now in Christian fellowship for joyous celebration. Let our outreach to others be expressed in the gifts we share from our hearts and from our hands. May the light of Christmas be seen in a mellowed glow of service that will permeate our lives in the coming year. Help us to accept fully the great gift of thy Son, Jesus, as our most precious heritage from the beloved Christmas season. Amen.

BLESSING FOR A NEW YEAR EVENT

At the beginning of each New Year there is a special longing to feel the reassurance of blessings provided throughout the changing days of each progressing month. Sometimes informal Watch Night parties are organized for various age groups, or there may be one large gathering. Special music makes a lovely transition from the Christmas season to the varied events of the coming year. Always there is a special awareness of the help available through prayer. Here is a suggested blessing for a New Year event.

Dear God, our minds and hearts turn in two directions as we recall the many blessings of the past year and look ahead to anticipated blessings of the year just beginning. None of us can know what of joy or sorrow will come into our lives, but we are grateful for the reassurance that thou wilt be with us whatever the situation we face.

Hear our thanks for the lasting joys of precious memories that keep the past a part of the present. Help us so to live day by day that we may build new memories to bless the future with happiness. Let no opportunity for service escape our knowledge, as with eyes of love we survey our surroundings and the needs of our loved ones.

May this be a year in which our hearts are enlarged to embrace those who need assurance of thy love, and thus may we move forward serenely through days of fellowship with one another and with thee. Amen.

A BLESSING OF BENEDICTION

Even as blessings are needed to open meetings, sometimes there is a definite need for a blessing to close a meeting. This is particularly true of a series of events held during a convention, a study seminar, or a vacation camp. Here is a summarizing blessing for such situations.

Dear God, our hearts are filled with thanks for the joy and blessing of fellowship with great minds and spirits through personal contacts, letters, books, music, travel, and all the many opportunities afforded by our church. Forgive us the times we have failed to take advantage of what is available to us in our weekly Sunday services and various midweek events. Accept our thanks for the rewarding satisfaction of achievements, whether at small tasks or large. Above all, hear our gratitude for a growing knowledge of thee through the spiritual influence of church activities. Grant to each heart the blessing of thy enduring peace, that our lives may be a benediction of blessing to others. Amen.